The Pot of Earth and the Iron Pot

The Pot of Earth and the Iron Pot

Ruth McIlroy

Shearsman Books

First published in the United Kingdom in 2022 by
Shearsman Books Ltd
PO Box 4239
Swindon
SN3 9FN

Shearsman Books Ltd Registered Office
30–31 St. James Place, Mangotsfield, Bristol BS16 9JB
(this address not for correspondence)

www.shearsman.com

ISBN 978-1-84861-828-2

ACKNOWLEDGEMENTS
Some of these poems have appeared in the following publications:
Poetry Review; Poetry Ireland Review; The Manchester Review;
Shearsman magazine; *the next review; Guppy Primer* (smith|doorstop)*;*
Stramullion Publishing; Chapman; The Rialto; Brittle Star; Cake;
Philip Larkin/East Riding Poetry Competition Anthology; Ver Poets
Open Competition Anthology; Templar Anthology; York Literature Festival
Prizewinners Anthology; The Winchester Poetry Prize Anthology.

CONTENTS

1

2

3

4

1

I read that my job was to woo the reader

what is it that I can possibly tell you
being able to look you straight in the eye?

1. live your life as a beautiful construct
2. with my eye of a cold magpie

(it doesn't matter how you say it
you could ice it on a cake
for all the difference it would make)

3. remember you are nothing but a notion
4. and not in possession of what you talk of

(finding your voice
that's the kiss of death isn't it)

5. it's not always easy to find THE THING
STOP. LIM.ITED. PAP.ER [.STOP]

Shallow

I think I must be some kind of shallow girl
I can be pulled down in melancholy
something in me is fine anything
and forge briskly

the dog is shallow too
oh look here is something we will appreciate we say
it's annoying to be shallow
but what must it be to be an indifferent person?

I am not honest

I am not honest.

My heart is a walnut;
I know nothing.

I enjoy dozens of exotic holidays a year.
I'm a girl but I've just always loved a scrap.

Anyway.

I do not suffer fools;
I suffer larks.
I suffer a peck of Dull Rubbish.

I am nothing
if not.

I believe myself to have become a little brutal.
£904 is paid every month into my bank account.

I do not know how to pronounce Eurydice.

Go in go in baby

This is a tipsy topsy evening
my legs are like tree legs

I am over-excited like a wild-eyed child
I am certainly not doing what would be more helpful
this is this very large garden for me

I sit as the seabird
in my triangular hut
I spy with my little eye.

A meant thing to tell

A Stetson left a man
it was quite well worn it was a costume
with a red feather and silver stars it was an archangel

I was jolted still by the extreme Stetson
it was like a fist punch it was like a visitation
it was complete it was the gravitational centre

this is a meant thing to tell
I was nothing but around it I was joyous I was savage
my perfect Stetson I do not have to replicate this

now I am bereft
and my true cowboy is bereft his Stetson
absent in Barnsley where the Sheffield Reds are playing
it'll be tasty a tidy match

absent your own Stetson you are lost
take me to the dance with my blood red varnish

For example I was in the sea at 4 a.m. today

and not one of the best parts of the sea around Southampton
I was under an oil refinery and the flame

it was opened in me that
I was not in the state to finding your voice
what a lot of things it exceeded to

a self collection occurred
lively but calmer I was out of available
satisfied of what sensations I tried

and everyone jumps into the turned-out-safe
that is stayedness and off you go we turned to me saying

Change of shift at the University Swimming Pool

The fact that suddenly as if he were in a chamber
and it was something like roofless
and his face was expressionless,
my swimming pool attendant, pool attendant
dumped his bag upon the table,
and if there could have been music
it would have been something deep and opening,
and I swam in the sacred lane for medium swimmers
barely knowing clockwise from anti-clock,

and he would put himself down as a cipher
in so far as this was none of his doing,
this twisting in on itself shedding strangeness
and I swam in a sacred hall partaking of sacredness.

I was running round the local park

and thought: today I'm running like a machine
stab stab my thighs on dirt track stomping
cold air through twin chambers minimum
double-tanking fuss and fankle

I was happy being machine
when round the bend beside a stream
was birdsong happening in the trees

o may this touch me through my stainless steel
why not why not I added as my piping.

Around/In

when I walk in town
I am along with my fingernails

my hair rides too   above and behind me
so   apart from clothes
it is just two keys
which are not integral
but always come too

one makes my car go
it is the magic doorway to me going around
like a person with superpowers I go from here to over there

the other lets me in to safety when I have done with going around

without the metal I could be out but not going around
caught out stock still stark naked in the open

when I am still, I wish to be *in*
as there, naturally, I cannot be got

when I am not in I head for this and for that
metal ably in service.

I was under an oil refinery and the flame

I was in the sea over wide and amongst
toward, under-tow
heavy smashing
equally wild and no intent

salt fill my mouth my
inhabit from
muscle open throat by thorax
belly by shoulder
expanse of waves from where
the sea was un   in all its

I was under an oil refinery
the refinery was present; it was before
complete unglinting   true
the refinery was dense but heavy
straight stood
(meant but bounded)
I saw lines
it did not waste

I was under an oil refinery and the flame
clean from dirty
excellent innocent flare
the flame was true
it had no

Will you be my bridesmaid

think happy thoughts!
because you are best over the other ones ha ha

making the world a more cheerful place
one colourful accessory at a time

shall we call the bestest man 'waspish'
or 'of a certain age',
let's maybe also call him 'formidable'
ha ha

don't be dull
join your random load of bollocks with mine
our girlish secrets

and if you are unwilling
I will leave you alone at a different table
and I will laugh with my mates
and you will have no mates

you are
the jewel
in my

The landscape of the heart is within the body cavern'd

I walked with regard to the tree
I navigated a path by means of it
stood in singular point

the field transfixed me the particular field
its hollows surface the field can
change or stay the same throughout time
see how deep the land goes what the river weighs

how to measure the carved hill
carving a particular arc and no other?
did you know that a curve which turns the heart
is described by its curvature and torsion?

a tilt describes a particular movement in time
the arc of a neck turned, golden light shaping

and why should lack not have a heart?
a heart within the body cavern'd

I see the distant path of crows
vectors; my mind says – *vectors of their flight.*
No. Concentrate. The world is
is not strange enough the tilting world.

Out of the woods

I wish I were
coherent more

this year I am
clear of   bare

the moon is bare
Girl, that were

a right big moon. Staring you were

was already

half-way there

after a dream

in which I was getting caught out leaving something innocuous
                                        in a strange woman's house
I woke up with a German accent
and it had snown.

One-trick pony

you a one-trick pony
hoof me once too many
me out of here

oh, did love you
had your back
you never had mine

did good for you
but you kick up stour
frisky one thing but was more

have to crash up, chuck and stir
clods and mud and rubble shower

me the one end up in mire

I'm not let you mucky me

have your head

there
I free

you go
I win, you know

don't want to

better if
we warm in stable
tar you hoof
comb you mane you muzzle

2

Theme – [melt
no melting]

one vainly shoring up buildings which refuse to be shored
one wandering aimlessly in the city of the spectacularly beautiful and
          impressive water

they change or stay the same through time they are the whole world
                    and everything we name
how extraordinary they are
'live your life as a beautiful building'

your life is a beautiful building it is hard to go further
shows that you are unfortunately your spirit it is hard to go further
but this does not relate to you it is hard to go further.

Theme – [heart
close]

'What was the center but the tower itself?'

It is on the verge of being too late, that took the road towards my heart
that it will notice and finally feel, turn and open, very grateful I came
        here and went home.

But the heart is deliberately blind it is a house that may or may not give
        you access
I do not even see waiting at the door.

The heart is unrecognisable as a house, a blacksmith, a furnace, a
        chapel, a mammal, a room with persecutors or resources
I circle it hopefully, confounded, the heart is silent. In the body's house
is the centre hidden, hidden, in a secret room? Hide, or in

or in the dead space, the flowering of last year has become a shell.

The quality state of the heart is easy to shine; it is an asset to reuse, or
                                an attractive and eye-catching product
easy to betray. Easy to betray by. Easy to stop holding it, pulling on a
                        fragile string that it is not too late.
Easy to walk away in wickedness and relief, to fight realistically.

By the way, there is no decision here, by the way. It is not true
that striving will be long and hard enough to lead to heart resumption
this may not be the case for the game you are playing against the odds

there is no way to know. Flash of sudden understanding/explanation is
        not stipulated.
Your journey may be fruitless. You may explore without fruit.

You do not know that.
You do not know the limits of people you do not know about the theme
of your heart.

You can grasp the heart out of the corner of your eye as you walk away
once you turn your back, your heart may decide by looking at you

can you turn your back on the right moment and know how to turn
your back and get wisdom at the correct speed and pace?

Please try again. The heart may be a formal garden.

Theme – [
exhaust]

I have reduced my price to free me

there was something exhausted
there was mistaken

flee the mine it is exhausted
flee the dead horse

the stone fallen out of my ring
it was a catastrophe I keen and laugh

and it was precious
gone finger empty for the miracle

The way he kept driving

Listen.
The third man is on watch.
(His fellow soldiers are in the hut manning the phoneline.)
He is at the east sandbag fortification
within the Ardboe compound,
and the sodium lights are pointing outwards,
illuminating the fields around him
and the waters of Lough Neagh.
It is 1972.
'It was quite romantic' he says laughingly,
'except it was just us three.'

The first time, someone must have taken a pot shot,
because no-one could have seen him through the sodium glare.
He saw the flash
and heard the *ping* on the chain-link fence,
and it missed him by 10 feet or so.
The second time, it missed him by even more,
but from the angle, they must have been in a boat,
which he found more disturbing.

The third time, another day,
the third man had a mortar fired at him
from the back of a flat-bed lorry,
an event which had its comic aspects, he said,
not least the dustbin they used,
and the pantomime puff of smoke,
and the way he kept driving towards the lorry
even after the shot had landed and gone off.

The Coffin Lift, Drumsheugh Nursing Home

Here is a concentration of death.
Coffin within coffin, like Chinese boxes
imagined in outline in this oblong,
so the mind shuns, yet knows
exactly how they lay, and at which precise angle
their edges rim your knees like cool water.

Daily they were slotted in this space
and slowly fell; the confluence of years
carved out the figure of their passing
to give this place a serious core,
in geometry which haunts me now
as lips of weirs and their glassy fall,
making of this shape a quiet memento
as knee-deep in death I rise.

DSM IV

(The DSM IV Diagnostic Manual classes
Personality Disorders under Axis II)

P e r s o n a l i t y
L i s t e n a r o p y
P e r s o n l a i t y
S t r i p y a l o n e
A y e n o r s p l i t.

I am called to a field of beneficence,
a field multi-axial, across five dimensions.
If I am to be haltlose, haughty, histrionic,
prithee then, let me be Axis II.

I dwell in a field of beneficence,
Deploying chameleon-like social skills.
There's many a notion in public works
specifically meant for me.

Praise me! PRAISE ME! **P**rovocative **R**elationships
Attention **I**nfluenced **S**peech **E**motional
Makeup **E**xaggerated. *I do I do this?*
(Numerous other strategies are used.)

I am placed in a field of beneficence,
an environment experienced as invalidating.
Mercurial disorder; I dwell on the border,
Oh folie maniaco; oh, folie! said he.

He's a loosely-conceived designation,
Experiencing disregulation,
Amygdalaic activation,
And melancholique ideation,

And overly passionate notions,
And slowly-subsiding emotions.

I am called to a field of beneficence.
And I am greatly loved.
And I am deeply grateful for my life.

Listen! A ropy
Person: laity?
Stripy, alone –

Aye, nor split.

The Judas song

Richard Strauss, who served under Hitler,
'warmed to him', and returned to form.
Here's to traitors; let's hear it for turncoats,
doing their stuff while the principled burn.

Give me a Stasi, a weak double-crosser;
oh I'm a one for collaborators, me.
There, by the grace of god – yes, *by*, you rhymesters,
pariahs, and two-faced informers – go we.

Easter Saturday

After the darkness, there is a time of waiting.
It is all we know of, or have,
and so we collect stones unhurriedly;
Iona marble, cool as egg
stretches out the moment with its whiteness,
stretching out our poverty for the sun to curl
on this salt unbearable richness.

This is enough; perhaps some day there will be
a place with better light, but now
I recognise your desire to stay
beside this thin abandoned sea
where at least it is quiet and calm
and wonderfully warmer than yesterday.

This did not make him feel like Buddha

on a visit to go on out and out wildly
he found instead an absence

he realised he was a house and had no rooms

and wanting to do something different, though frightening
he left up the glen

and in lovely doubt, in relieved surrender
he took himself to the tarn

for a moment –

dismay to his bones
dismay through him
dismay to his muscles

then –

everything goes through as I walk, he thought
I am one of many things / I am not
noting that this did not make him feel like Buddha,
he was not quiet nor quiet

He feels too old to be interesting

he thinks he is too old to improve himself
he will not be cheated into

he will recognise anxious and say 'anyway, they cannot do anything
        about you, I'll live happily anyway'
that's enough chewing

he does not understand the temptations to do musings
how little he immerses himself
in melodic thoughts that are nurtured to fill his head

the decline in the world is amazing
some of you will not be able to live happily and anywhere

for what are the ways he will seek in the streets of old age in the heavens
        or on the road, a drink in the sun or of the city.

Spider brain tally

I left a kilo of squirrel in the gutter

but what about the bucket of spiders I've saved this year –
will one or any of them step up or stand by me?

thirty forty spider brains twinking in my garden
all because of me, my rescue spiders

not to mention all the other
little animal centres;
who will map or audit the prickle of brains, bee, aphid
brown ant, beetle, teeming unseen, outside?

now, when I walk
I walk this brainscape
step on a brain
we swallow brains
even vegans
even Jains!

I need to be clean and spare to write of spiders and their distribution.
Their livingness submerges me.
I cannot bear their mass or their corporeality.

I have appointed myself Chief Counter of the Brains
Citizen Spider Mrs Aphid
Dame Ant.

settle

settle the poem it is not going anywhere
the moon is a harvest moon and therefore or also red

the moon is out of reach being outside, whereas inside one can settle

inside the capacious house I settled
paid obeisance to my footfall around the planks look   look
at the path taken between my door and my table

taken up space

albeit extraneous factors arise that is
outside, a horseman and his gallant nag 'ride towards Death'

ah duende

why does the man go forward
why does he not settle?

give up little horseman it is better to hunker
the little black pony needs to be settled

settle the pony, it is not going anywhere
stable warm coat muzzle.

Undo your heart

My name is Millie Small,
I come from Finger Post,
I do not come to boast,
but I come to be a young lady.

My heart is quite undone,
but I am young.

The art of the perfect gift

I will be making further purchases.
I now have a very happy wife!
Solid bronze.

And what a figure,
Beautifully boxed. Thank you.

The hare has been delivered as promised.

Fionnphort Crossing

Iain MacGillivray, the captain and owner
of Pride of the Hebrides, a one-car ferry
(the pride consisting of taking her out
whatever the weather, between Fionnphort and Iona),

talked of the four young lads going home
over the same strait only last summer
using their own sturdy boat, but had taken a few,
and just the one made it, he said, and so on;

so when you clung on, and clamped your eyes shut,
and begged me to say the waves had got smaller,
in that rusty old skip, excuse for a ferry,
and the mountainous seas over us on both sides,

and I said we were safe, and I lied, and I lied,
and you later proclaimed I'd stepped up to the mark,
well, it wasn't like that; for you still do not know
of the deep laugh that swelled up, that swelled up inside.

Four treasures
(Fjouwer trekken)

I forgot to them
ik ha fergetten dat ik se hie

then I did not know what were
ik wist net dat

then I did not know to do
en ik wist net wat mei har te dwaan

then I asked them what shall do
(then I asked what shall I)
en ik frege

no answer gijn antwurd
(came through)

3

Prayer of the pauper

That the bones which you have broken may rejoice (Psalm 51:8)

Into your hands, O Lord, I commend my spirit.
Hide me under the shadow of your wings;
forgive me my necessary budgetings.

For we are the bones, broken and scattered, are we not,
lying cheerfully and stumpily around,
clattering quietly at each other's processes,
peace settling on us, against all reason.

Injunctions to the hesitant

Get ready. Get steady. Then go.
Start when you're ready,
go when you're steady,
and never repeat; and don't miss a beat,
gather ye rosebuds while you may,
don't tarry along that road. Sweet day!

So cool, so calm, so bright; but stop;
to plagiarise is not an option
in the place you've landed up,
this kingdom of the half-filled cup –

glorious, glorious cup half-full,
go tell it to the mountain, rule
the dum-de-dumming of this land
and and and and, and and and – and

Aims of the Zoo Questionnaire's Survey

The first question ('Name of zoo:' and 'Country:')

Question 2 ('What diet (food & nutrients)
do you feed the aardvarks in your zoo?')

Question 2a ('Do you sometimes feed them food scraps
(as sometimes pigs are fed with)?')
Question 2b ('How do you feed the food?') was asked
in the hope that some zoos would use a fake termite-mound.

Question 3 ('What seems to be the purpose?')
should then help to understand why aardvarks swim at all.

Guppy Primer

I

Beautiful Guppies don't just happen.
The secret is *sweat*, and attention to detail.
Treat them to good live food when you pass them from the left,
And siphon off 10% of their water when you pass them from the right.
Replace the water with aged good water, such as Bronx, NY
Tap water, which has a pH of 6.8.

Be sure to throw away the bad males, and before long
You'll have a tank of beautiful Guppies.

Learn to watch out for unscrupulous dealers
Who sell fancy males with common females.
Look out for babies hiding among the plants.
Guppies drop babies every 28 days or so.
Put them immediately in the breeding trap you bought
In anticipation of the Blessed Event.

(The best reason for providing a breeding trap is illustrated
By this photograph showing a female Guppy eating her young.)

Your purpose here is to end up with some virgin females;
Try to keep your babies sorted out according to sex.
Some of the females can go back in with their parents
To breed with their father or uncle, or be crossed
With their brothers in separate miniature jars.

Keep inbreeding your fish for a few generations;
This is the way new varieties spring up.

Breed those fish you like the best
With the virgin females.

But check the virgins first.

II

I have seen the same Guppy sold
By four different people under four different names.
Hahnel's red Guppies, for example:

Flamingo Guppies; Flame Guppies;
Redtail Guppies; Fire Guppies;
Red Ruby Guppies; Whore Guppies;
Leopard Guppies; Green Guppies;
Swordtail Guppies; Veiltail Guppies;
English Golden Lacetail Guppies.

Beautiful Guppies don't just happen.

All that

He made some big mistakes; he sold the sandwich bar
the year before the office blocks began to open.
The neighbourhood had been re-zoned commercial; he must have heard.

Back on the airport taxis, he'd invent life-stories
until one day a passenger said 'We were in your cab last week'.
After that he grew a big fat stomach, putting it down to boredom.

The man's life was full of holes. Sweet basil grew along his windowsill,
garlic from the Halal store, his table spread with onions,
plum tomatoes, parmigiana, olive oil from Lucca.

'You know what would pay round here,' he'd say, 'dog-walking.
'Walking people's dogs for money. But will he listen?
'Useless, that boy of ours, no effing use at all.'

Getting a start in farming

anyone would think it would be nigh-on impossible to set up farming
        round here
well they'd be wrong

here's my pigs, a lovely fatty breed
they have to be crossed with a more modern breed

if you want to get the size
and you want to get the sausages out

only the bigger animals have sausages inside them when you open them up
these guys will go orf down to a local abattoir and then they will return

and we sell pork, lamb and beef in chunks
so we sell either a quarter of or half of a pig *oink oink*

we label them, we allocate them to all the different
then we deliver them on Wednesday

I take a white van, that van
I wear my white coat and my hat

and my white wellies and orf I go
and I go to Bristol and Bath and then up to London

there were twenty-six cows and twenty six sheep
we hardly knew the difference when we began
we also sell live heifers surplus to our requirements
all of the animals going round all of the fields one after the other.

Some masts

*(Poles of Inaccessibility exist on each landmass, marking the furthest point
from the ocean; and in each ocean, marking the furthest point from the land)*

The Oceanic Pole of Inaccessibility
is the most strange Pole and often the nearest human being
is astronaut (258 miles to International Space Station
1670 miles from the land)
Space junk's dump
"Spaceship Cemetery"

We have not reached the Arctic Pole of Inaccessibility
no one has ever decided where it is
except that it shifts everywhere in the middle of nowhere

The North American Pole of Inaccessibility
is in an unmarked gully
between Allen and Kyle South Dakota

Inaccessible Southern Pole was visited by the Soviets
they saw the earthquakes and observed glaciers and stars
alone for 40 years a hut was buried in the ice but one could see the location
by the bust of Lenin placed there by the Soviet Union and some masts

Gaps
(to the tune of Streets of Laredo)

One night, at a lighthouse, I crept out to star-gaze;
I didn't remember the circling beam.
I sat on the bench and looked up at the heavens.
(Constellations - then nothing - constellations – the beam).

As I felt my way back by the curve of the sea-wall
It was,   , stars,   ,stars,   , stars,   ;
And to fill in the gaps then my brain took a fancy
(There was dream   not dream, beam not beam, dream   not dream, beam).

It pulled out some scraps of old song-lines and sayings
On the tip of my tongue; yes, like that, no, not that.
And I watched them come streaming, my dear higher functions,
Stuttering on in the dark; let them run, let them run.

Old man with cane and Panama

for P.K.M 1930–2010

I was shoulder deep in the sea at Coney Island
when I saw you stepping down the beach,
singular and content.

I love to see you unencumbered.
You knew me from the others in the sea;
your steady look said 'What is this to me?'

I remembered winter; how we closed your eyes.
I thought that you were gone forever.
And now I hope, with a child's unreason.

Stay; don't stay, dear father; hold me
longer in your enigmatic gaze,
mild, unbending, in the Southern Brooklyn haze.

You turned and walked back up the beach;
the ocean held my arms down by my sides,
rocking me in the long Atlantic swell.

The jets roared over towards Newark, or JFK.

From *De la Causa, Principio e uno* (1584)
Giordano Bruno

Cavallier of the order of the Most Christian King,
conseglier of his private Conseglio, captain of 50 men,
and ambassador to the Queen of England Serenissima,
reviled by knaves and persecuted by genii bestial, loved by savii,
       admirato by scholars,
magnified by large, estimated to be powerful and favored by the gods;
I, for this much favor from you already ricettato
nodrito, defended, delivered, felt safe, kept in port,
escaped to you from perilous and mighty storm,
consecrate to you this anchor, these seamstresses, these fiaccate sails.

If all forms are contained as from that,
and the same by virtue of the efficient (on what can be indistinct
       likewise from her second being)
produced and parturite; and who have not less than
raggione attualità nell'essere sensitive and explicit, though not according
       to accidental existence, being
that everything you see and Fassi open for accidents based on the size,
it is pure accident; remaining still the Substance detects and identifies
coincident with the matter. Waves, it is quite clear
that dall'esplicazione we can not take anything but damn the fate that
       sustanziali differences are occolte,
said Aristotle forced from the truth.

Stance

From Musashi's Book of Five Rings

Adopt a stance with the head erect,
Neither hanging down, nor looking up, nor twisted.
Your forehead and the space between your eyes

Should not be wrinkled. Do not roll your eyes
Nor allow them to blink, but slightly narrow them.
Keep the line of your nose straight, slightly flaring your nostrils.

Hold the line of the rear of the neck
Straight. Instil vigour into your hairline.
Lower both shoulders, put strength in your legs

From the knees to the tips of your toes.
Make the everyday stance your combat stance.
The gaze should be large and broad.

It is important to know the enemy's sword
And not be distracted by insignificant movements.
When you cannot be deceived by men

You will have realised the wisdom of strategy.
Your spirit should be settled, yet unbiased;
Do not let the enemy see your spirit.

The Way of Strategy

From Musashi's Book of Five Rings

When I reached thirty, I looked back on my past.
My victories had little to do with strategy;
More to the order of heaven perhaps; or natural ability,

Or the others' inferior strategy. I resolved
To master strategy, and studied morning and night.
I came to the Way of Strategy when I was fifty.

Since then I have lived without following any particular Way.
Thus, with the virtue of strategy, I practice
Many arts and abilities – all with no teacher.

If you want to learn of this Way, consider these things
One at a time; you must do sufficient research.
I cannot write in detail how this is done.

To write this poem I did not use the law of Buddha,
Or the teachings of Confucius. It is the night of the tenth day
Of the tenth month, at the hour of the tiger.

The Pot of Earth and the Iron Pot

The Iron Pot proposed a trip, to the Pot of Earth.
She excused herself, saying "I would be wise
to keep the corner of the fire, for it needs so little, so
little, the slightest thing for me to go to debris,
and would not come back.

"For you," said she, "whose skin is harder than mine,
I do not see a thing that will hold you back".
"I'll put you under cover" replied the Iron Pot.
"If some hard stuff threatens you with adventure,
between the two of you will I pass,
and suddenly I you will save."

This offer persuades her. Iron Pot, her comrade,
gets right at her side. Clopin-clopant as they can,
one against the other thrown, at the slightest hiccup
they tremble. The Pot of Earth she suffers;
she had not taken a hundred steps
than by her companion she was shattered.

Let us associate only with our equals,
or we will have to fear the fate of one of these pots.

The Hare and the Turtle

There is no point running; we must start at the right time.
The Hare and the Turtle are a testimony.
"Let's wager" said the latter, "that you will not reach
As soon as me this goal." – And so was done.

Our Hare had only four steps to go,
Having, I say, some rest time to graze,
To sleep, and to listen where does the wind come from.
It left the Turtle go on her stately train.

She leaves, she does it. She is hurrying slowly.
The Hare, however, despises such a victory,
Holds the wager to little glory,
Believes that there is honour to leave late. He grazes,
He rests, he's having fun with everything else.
What a challenge. In the end, when he sees
That the other was almost at the end of her career,
He leaves like a line; but the impulses he makes are vain.

The Turtle arrived first. "Well," she cried, "was I not right?
What does your speed serve you? Me, I win!
And what would it be if you were wearing a house?"

Mon in the moon

mon stan and stri'
bear burden but
much wonder at he's na downslidden
dootin hissel he shiver shaken

freeze frost he chilly
thorns make tatty
when he sit?
or know his clothes?

whery think the way he take?
he set un foot aft un tother
nothin make him not no hurry
he the slowest mon that ever was

up on heh whenever he were got
he were in that moon begot and fed
lean he on his stick like a fat friar
crock-idler – sore he is adread

mony a day go by that is he here
I think his errand he not as no speed
I think he owe a pretty penny
he know not what

'mon if you owe get go
drink wit the one who lend to you
when he drunk as a drunken kitten
you he will let off – is true

'mon hear me out
hup forth! o chump as art
I know tha got one bellyfull.
he deaf? then hell wit he

that I hey-hey up nowt he hurry
the lost less lad no have no clue
tho he he make my teeth go aiee
he not be down till morning day.

Mary Queen of Scots, when an Infant,

stripped by Order of Mary of Guise, her Mother, to convince Sadler, the English Ambassador, that she was not a Decrepit Child, which had been Insinuated at Court.

it is difficult to argue that this painting
with its cramped stagey effects

– rework the heads –
that this painting is one of them

dear child
dear, decrepit child

4

Just idiot talk

"Hey, Sassenach! Ye gie me the boak,
Yir patter stinks; youse'll get it noo,
Ye cannae say a'thing, ya muckle-face numpty".

But, ya wee keelie, I'll jist dae it efter.
Missed yersel' there now, eh no, hen?
Ken, this's barry, nae tother a ba'.

Glossary

Just idiot talk	*Just an idiolect consciously employed to gain acceptance from a dominant social group*
Hey, Sassenach	Excuse me, English person
ye gie me the boak	you make me feel nauseous
Yir patter stinks	your way of presenting yourself to the world is fundamentally flawed
youse'll get it noo	you (singular or plural) are about to experience retribution
ye cannae say a'thing	I would advise you not to answer me back
ya muckle-face numpty	you ill-favoured person of limited common sense
But, ya wee keelie	But, you young person from a challenging home environment
I'll jist dae it efter	I'll just do it later
Missed yersel' there now	you didn't see that one coming
eh no, hen?	did you, my friend/acquaintance
ken, this's barry	you know something, I feel a lot better
nae tother a ba'	no bother at all

To Tricky Margaret, who had spread
a slanderous account of the poetess

No, Margaret, you trickster, why did you spread one wrong story
that a babe who was not baptized was in my womb;
why not pronounce the truth as surely as I do?
Not alike my father, you slanderer and yours.
Not equal were my brothers and your unlovely louts.
Not alike were our homes.
Bones of wild venison were found in my father's house;
in your father's house were bree, and fish bones your fare.
As I climb from the town, my step is heavy and reserved.
I am ill-pleased with the hussy who hatched that lie story,
the basest refuse of the folk, a light jade without cattle.

Lament for Seathan

My love Seathan, you are a gentle sight;
many a glen and ben have we traversed.
I have lain beside you on a narrow bed,
a bed of heather and stone on stone.

I slept a night on a sea-rock with you,
I did, my love, and I did not regret it.
Wrapped in a corner of your homely plaid,
the sea-spray ever breaking over us;
water that is very pure, cool and wholesome.

Alas! Now Seathan is in the upper gaol
and I am restless on my pillow.
He has nobody that pities him
but me, who is running to and fro.

If I could but ransom my love Seathan
I would not leave a cow in the field,
neither the black cow nor the red,
nor herds of the fine white-shouldered cattle,
of the long-horned, white-backed, red-eared cattle.

The Vixen

Catherine's the wench
    churlish and haggard,
ill-favoured, scrawny,
    ungainly, perverse:
I pray each morning
    to the Choir of Angels
for relief from the harpy,
    wilful and thrawn,
that she be not hale,
    nor live long, nor prosper!

I pray each evening,
    both Sundays and weekdays,
that the harridan be stowed
    with the graveyard rabble:
may the lives be shortened
    of herself and her people,
her goats and her sheep,
    her beasts and her kine –
be they pillaged and plundered,
    be they blighted and felled!

On her flocks be canker
    baneful, unwholesome,
scrapie and maggots,
    dysentery, flux:
be they poisoned by venom,
    be they ravaged by wolves,
by curs, red foxes,
    and murderous hounds.

I pray each hour
    to the Throne of Grace
that she and her cattle
    be wretched and luckless:
to Catherine no sons,

no calf to her cows,
no plumpness, no solace,
    no comely look, fairness,
but each night and day
    doleful and graceless.

Let her summers be short,
    bleak and unfavourable,
her winters be long,
    unsparing with cold,
her springs be frost-bound,
    wearisome, arduous,
her autumns be squally,
    inclement and cheerless,
storm-ridden, calamitous,
    lamentable, foul.

Sharpening outward,
    shortening inward,
ruin to southward,
    ruin to northward,
eastward and westward,
    be hers for ever!

Ruin from below,
    ruin from above,
ruin from on high,
    ruin from beneath,
ruin be east of her,
    ruin be west,
ruin be south of her,
    ruin be north:
the ruin of the seven
    miserable ruins
till the end of time
    I ask be hers!

A charm with yarrow

I will choose yarrow and yarrow will delight my elegant fingers warmer

my lips are the juice of six strawberries, in the sea I am an island
and on the land I am a hill and when the moon disappears, I am a star

and I am a staff to you when you are weak, and my lips are warmer
and warmer and I can love a bird out of a tree and I choose yarrow yarrow.

Invocation of grace

Rock of the yellow
on the king's white daughter,
the gleam of the eye,
a sweetheart of love.

A sea you travel
and you will return;
you are the light,
the star of the morning.

Lance and arrow,
the ax of the bull,
bloom of the sword
protect you.

Copper of the stone,
bronze of the gold,
gold of silver
protect you.

Travelling past
small steading,
great town,
seaweed and land,

you see, you govern,
land of the land,
sea of the land,
my heart, my face.

My croft of music,
every dream you live,
every intention of life is to live.

Jealousy

A plaint by Màiri nighean Ruaidh, deceived by her lover.

Oh, oh, oh,
it is I that have got a sore heart,
there is a loch of tears under my pillow.

Though I will go to bed,
no sleeping for me
while yon Islay woman brings jealousy into my heart,

who took my sweetheart from me
that I would choose above one hundred others.

No, but if I were before her
there would be ripping of kerchiefs.

Though I be away from the town, my love,
far from home and dejected,
it is not seemly that this Islay woman beset you.

The Omen

Early on the morning of a Monday,
A lamb heard bleating,
And a bird meadow,
And blue-blue cuckoo,
And no food on my stomach.

The fair morning of Tuesday,
On the smooth stone
A snail, slimy, wan.
And the ashy wheatear
On the top of the hollow,
The foal of the old mare
Of lively gait, and its back to me.
I knew from these
That the year would not go well.

Exorcism of the eye

Salt in the face,
How do you put a lamb on blade,
As you burn on burn,
How do you go to sea-hog,
As the army was going,
How will the army go?

I have plenty of rain,
I have a heather,
I have a fire on it,
I have plenty of sorrow,
I have strong strength,
I am very clear,
I have the strength of my cell,
I have the strength of my spear,
The strength of heaven.

Thread on the top of the green,
One third on the beaches,
Shingle on the brine.

Incantation I

(From the Scottish Gaelic)

Haar; bride out
Early morning
Horse with a friend
Horse broke his leg.
With much ado
That was apart
She put backbone to backbone
She put flesh to flesh
She put gullet to gullet
She put vein to vein.
As she is healing
I have this healing.

Incantation II (Charm against the rose)

Rose death-like, deadly, swollen,
Leave the udder of the cow,
Leave the udder of the cat-heads,
Leave, leave that to single peat
And cross to single peat not you.

A stubborn rose, thrawn,
When cow udder,
Leave the pastry and the udder,
Flee to stone.

I place rose with stone,
I place stone to the stone floor,
I place milk in the udder,
I place substance in the kidney.

Incantation III

Third on the lawn of aesthetic,
The third is great dirty sea,
She herself is the best instrument to carry it,
  A great sea dirty,
  A great salt sea.

The name of the Tri Dull,
The name of the Tri Numh,
The name of Nan Uile Run,
The name of the Great Powers.

She herself is the best instrument to carry it,
  A great sea dirty,
  A great salt sea,
The best instrument to carry it.

These are the ways I have made my ruin

It was then spoke the sorrowing woman
these are the ways I have made my ruin

once I would walk the salty shore
with neither grace nor lack of grace
unclothed of skill I was singing
I had no attention to spare for artifice

then I became afraid of abandon
I would fear the love of birdsong
I did not delight in the smell of hawthorn
or the sun rising over the loch

I have not been true
and I come to the end of my days
crushed and cold as the ditch

drive the liar from my house
rather let me seek the genuine prayer
and water from the eyelids flowing swiftly

Acknowledgements and Notes

p. 15 **For example I was in the sea at 4 a.m. today**
after Philip Hoare RISINGTIDEFALLINGSTAR

p. 19 **I was under an oil refinery and the flame**
Acknowledgement to Philip Hoare

p. 54 **Some masts**
Acknowledgements to smithsonian.com (Kat Escher); BBC (Ella Davis)

p. 60/61 **The Pot of Earth and the Iron Pot**
          The Hare and the Turtle
After Fables*, Jean de la Fontaine, 1668*

p, 62 **Mon in the moon**
after The man in the Moon, late 13th / early 14th century anonymous English Lyric

p. 64 **Mary Queen of Scots, when an Infant…**
Benjamin Robert Haydon 1842 (oil on canvas)

p. 68 **To Tricky Margaret…**
after 'A Satirical Song', in Gaelic Songs of Mary Macleod; The Matheson Collection.

p. 69 **Lament for Seathan**
p. 70-71 **The Vixen**
Acknowledgements to A Carmichael, Carmina Gadelica

p. 72 **A charm with yarrow**
after A Charm with yarrow (Scottish Gaelic, traditional folk charm)

p. 73 **Invocation of grace**
p. 74 **Jealousy**
p. 75 **The Omen**
p. 76 **Exorcism of the Eye**
p. 77 **Incantation 1**

Acknowledgements to Carmina Gadelica